Little Pebble™

T0052270

MIGHTY MILITARY MACHINES

Aircraft Carriers

by Matt Scheff

PEBBLE
a capstone imprint

Little Pebble is published by Pebble
1710 Roe Crest Drive, North Mankato,
Minnesota 56003
www.mycapstone.com

Copyright © 2019 by Pebble, a Capstone imprint. All rights reserved. No part of this publication may be reproduced in whole or in part, or stored in a retrieval system, or transmitted in any form or by any means, electronic, mechanical, photocopying, recording, or otherwise, without written permission of the publisher.

Library of Congress Cataloging-in-Publication Data
Names: Scheff, Matt, author.
Title: Aircraft carriers : a 4D book / by Matt Scheff.
Description: North Mankato, Minnesota : Pebble, [2018] |
Series: Little pebble. Mighty military machines |
Audience: Ages 4–8.
Identifiers: LCCN 2018004136 (print) |
LCCN 2018006808 (ebook) |
ISBN 9781977101259 (eBook PDF) |
ISBN 9781977101136 (hardcover) |
ISBN 9781977101198 (paperback)
Subjects: LCSH: Aircraft carriers—Juvenile literature.
Classification: LCC V874 (ebook) |
LCC V874 .S35 2018 (print) | DDC 623.825/5—dc23
LC record available at https://lccn.loc.gov/2018004136

Editorial Credits
Marissa Kirkman, editor; Heidi Thompson, designer; Jo Miller, media researcher; Tori Abraham, production specialist

Photo Credits
U.S. Navy Photo by MC2 Paul L. Archer, 9, MC3 Anthony J. Rivera, 7, MC3 Ignacio D. Perez, 11, MCSN Erika Kugler, 15, Casey J. Hopkins, cover; Wikimedia: U. S. Navy photo by MCSN Brandon Morris, 17, MC3 Anderson W. Branch, 21, MC3 Justin M. Smelley, 19, MCSA Rachel N. Clayton, 13, MCSN Lauren Booher, 5
Design Elements: Shutterstock: Zerbor

Printed in the United States 5572

Table of Contents

Big Ships 4

At Sea 8

Parts. 14

Glossary 22

Read More 23

Internet Sites 23

Critical Thinking Questions . . . 24

Index. 24

Big Ships

Look! A plane is landing.

It is on an aircraft carrier.

A carrier is a navy ship.

It is big.

It carries planes.

At Sea

The ship is at sea.

It is like an airport.

Pilots fly the planes.

The crew fixes them.

pilot
crew

The planes take off.

They land.

102
300

Parts

This is the hull.

It is the ship's body.

It is made of steel.

hull

Engines power the ship.

They make it go.

65
E

The flight deck is big.

It is flat.

Planes land on it.

Boom! Blast!

The ship has guns.

Glossary

airport—a place where aircraft take off and land

crew—a team of people who work together

engine—a machine that makes the power needed to move something

flight deck—the long, flat area on top of an aircraft carrier where planes can take off and land

hull—the main body of a boat or ship

navy—the branch of the military that fights on water

steel—a strong type of metal

Read More

Boothroyd, Jennifer. *Inside the US Navy*. U.S. Armed Forces. Minneapolis: Lerner Publications, 2017.

Reed, Jennifer. *The U.S. Navy*. The U.S. Military Branches. North Mankato, Minn.: Capstone Press, 2018.

Willis, John. *Aircraft Carriers*. Mighty Military Machines. New York: AV2 by Weigl, 2017.

Internet Sites

Use FactHound to find Internet sites related to this book.

Visit *www.facthound.com*
Just type in 9781977101136 and go.

Check out projects, games and lots more at
www.capstonekids.com

Critical Thinking Questions

1. Where do airplanes land on an aircraft carrier?
2. What is the hull made of?
3. Which part gives an aircraft carrier its power?

Index

airports, 8
crew, 10
engines, 16
flight decks, 18
guns, 20
hulls, 14
pilots, 10
planes, 4, 6, 10, 12, 18
ships, 6, 8, 14, 16, 20
steel, 14